W9-CAS-917

RESTORATION OF
THE MODERN DAY
PROPHET

by D. Steven Schultz

Published and available through

Preparing The Way Ministries, Inc.
Steve & Eileen Schultz
P.O. Box 1711
Santa Rosa Beach, FL 32459

Distributed by

CHRISTIAN INTERNATIONAL
P.O. BOX 9000
SANTA ROSA BEACH, FL 32459
904-231-2600

Other books written by the author:
"Radical Warriors Require Radical Training"
"Mentoring and Fathering"

ISBN # 0-9624461-0-6

Scripture quotations are taken from the Authorized King
James Version

Let the prophets speak and may God grant us the grace to hear His voice in this very important hour. Amen

IN APPRECIATION

I would like to thank all the people who have made this publication possible. I owe a greăt debt of gratitude to my mentors, coaches, friends and family. As it has been said, "No man becomes anything without the help of others". I owe a special debt of gratitude to the following ministers and ministries who have willingly shared great prophetic truths: Bishop Bill Hamon and the staff of Christian International Ministries who continue to pioneer the prophetic move (and who have provided me with friendship, oversight, and covering); Dr. David Blomgren of Tampa Bay Christian Center, Brandon Florida; and to Apostolic team leader of Church Of The Nations International, Tony Fitzgerald. Also to those ministers who I have had the priviledge of co-laboring with in the Kingdom: Pastor David Deaton of New Covenant Fellowship, Ft. Myers, Florida; Jerry Lynde; Clement J. Ferris; and all the other ministers with whom I have had the honor to serve. A special thanks to James Trivette, Mevalene Peters and Ginny Cataldo for their editing and typesetting skills.

1) Covenant
- not Bucking I Cor 4:15
the ministry   Fathers

DEDICATION

The Apostle Paul's words in I Cor.4:15 so aptly states the condition of the Church today:

"For though ye have ten thousand instructors in Christ, yet have ye not many fathers:..."

At present, there are many young Elishas that are searching to find their Elijah. I have been blessed and privileged by the Lord to have found one of mine. Therefore, I dedicate this book to Bishop Bill Hamon, Founder and President of Christian International Ministries, who has so willingly accepted the difficult position as a "papa" prophet in the Body of Christ. His love for God's Church is evidenced by his dedication to train and relate to so many of the Lord's young prophets, and in his willingness to share prophetic insights gained through years of ministry experience.

disconnected
unplugged
Broken
even flow
twisted

RESTORATION OF THE MODERN DAY PROPHET

by D. Steven Schultz

TABLE OF CONTENTS

what people do not understand, they are against.

INTRODUCTION

The Apostle John stated that in the last days there would be a great increase in the "false anointing." We need to be a discerning people who recognize the true anointing and the Lord's true ministry gifts. There is an old adage which states, "What people do not understand, they are against."

My prayer and purpose for this small book is to help give you a greater appreciation and understanding of what the Lord is doing in this hour in regards to the present day rise of the New Testament prophet (Eph. 4:11) and his ministry. I trust that this small booklet will bring greater understanding on the prophet's role in the Church today.

Please keep in mind that this material is by no means an "in-depth" study of the prophet's ministry, for many volumes could be written, but I do trust that what is presented is balanced (Prov. 11:1). My heart's desire is that it will shed more light on what in the past has been a "mysterious" subject and that this publication will bless God's people, the Body of Christ.

CHAPTER ONE

THE PRESENT DAY RISE OF THE PROPHETIC

→ Prophet

"Woe to you, lawyers - experts in the Mosaic law! For you have taken away the key to knowledge; You did not go in yourselves, and you hindered and prevented those who were entering."

Luke 11:52

In Luke, chapter 11, we see Jesus Christ rebuking the lawyers of his day because they and their forefathers had "taken away the key to knowledge." The "key to knowledge" as referred to in this passage of scripture is the gifting and ministry of the prophet. The Old Testament prophet's role was to be a mouthpiece for God to the children of Israel so that God's people might walk upright and holy before Him. Today, the Lord is restoring back to the Church, (the New Testament Israel) the full anointing of the ministry of the prophet, so that the church will continue to grow to purity and maturity. **We are at a time in history when the world and the Church desperately need to hear from heaven.** The Bible clearly states that in the last days there will be many false teachers, false apostles and false prophets (I John 4:11; II Peter 2:1; II Cor. 11:13). To recognize the "false prophet", we must recognize, understand and appreciate one of the five gifts that Jesus gave to the Church - the true N.T. prophet. This gift ministry is close to the Father's heart (I Chron. 16:22 & Psalm 105:15) and is being amplified and revealed in this hour of the Church.

Church history reveals that God, in His sovereignty, has had seasons of restoration where He has accentuated and illuminated certain truths from the word of God. Acts 3:19 states that "times of refreshing shall come from the presence of the Lord," and that the "heavens must retain Jesus until the times of restoration of all things." There are different periods when God, in His infinite wisdom, chooses to release revelation knowledge to His Bride so that we might come closer to the image of Jesus Christ. Some of the past times of restoration have been classified below[1]:

DATE	MOVEMENT	REVELATION RESTORED
1500's	Protestant	Justification by Faith
1800's	Holiness	Sanctification
1900's	Pentecostal	Holy Spirit & His Gifts
1940's	Latter Rain	Laying on of Hands, Healing & Deliverance (Evangelist)
1960's	Charismatic	Unity, Demonology, (Teacher) Faith, Prosperity, (Pastor) "Word" Movement

[1] The Eternal Church by Dr. Bill Hamon, Christian International, 1981, Pgs. 158, 309

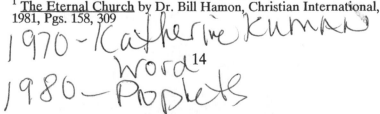

1970 - Katherine Kuhman

1980 - Prophets

Word[14]

As you can see from this very simple chart on church history, God is **progressively** restoring biblical truth in the heart of His people. **Every movement,** (also spoken of as "wave", "wind of the Spirit", "revival", etc.) **is produced by the Holy Spirit with one main intention; to reveal and establish truth to the Church, so that we might be conformed to the image of His Son, Jesus Christ** (Rom 8:29) **and to come to covenant family reality**. (Jn.17:21)

We see that in the early 1950's, the Holy Spirit brought illumination and understanding on the ministry of the evangelist. In the 1960's, the ministry of the pastor was enhanced, and in the 1970's, (with a great emphasis on "the Word"), the Lord raised many anointed teachers. For the first time in hundreds of years, the Body of Christ came to acknowledge, understand and appreciate God-called and equipped teachers. The decade of the 1980's was a transition time and a time when many began to hear the beat of a different drum. It was a decade when God was calling forth a company of N.T. prophets to be trained and released for the 1990's.

As the Spirit of God releases His anointed prophets to the Church in this hour, we must have an ear to hear what the Spirit is saying. The 1990's will be a decade of greater prophetic emphasis and apostolic restoration. Through the rise of the prophetic will come the recognition and release of a great apostolic company in the last of the last days.

15

The prophetic ministry is coming to the forefront in this hour, because God has ordained this time to reveal to His Church the "Elijah Company." Even as God sent John the Baptist to prepare the way for the Lord's first coming, He is now releasing a company of prophets who are coming in the spirit of Elijah to prepare the way for His second coming (Mal. 4:5, 6). We need to rejoice that we are the generation to whom God has chosen to restore the full anointing back to the prophetic call. Let the prophets speak and may God grant us the grace to hear His voice in this very important hour.

Mal 4:5+6

Leaders need to be doing these three things

CHAPTER TWO

WHY DO WE NEED THE N.T. PROPHET?

Titles   *5-fold*   *Eph 4:11-14*

Deacons

"And he gave some, apostles; and some, prophets; and some, evangelists; and some, pastors and teachers; for the (1) perfecting of the saints, for the (2) work of the ministry, for the edifying of the body of Christ." (3)

Ephesians 4:11,12

Everything God does, He does with a purpose. When we understand this principle, we come to the realization that with the restoration and illumination of the prophet's ministry, there is an important purpose. Ephesians 4:11 states that Jesus gave to the Church five "gifts", which are to be an integral and important part of bringing His Bride to perfection.

Most believers will readily accept and affirm that the ministry of the N.T. pastor is vital and necessary to the growth and development of the local church and the universal Church. They will also most likely recognize and accept two other ministry gifts; those of the evangelist and teacher. Many of these same Christians truly believe Ephesians 4:11; but, when asked if they under-

17

stand and can explain the N.T. prophet, there is usually little response. This is not to find fault with most believers; but, it is stated to explain that **there has been gross misunderstanding and mysticism in regards to the ministry gift of prophet.** The Church is slowly coming to the understanding of this vital gift sent by Jesus Christ.

We need the N.T. prophet's ministry today because the Apostle Paul clearly discloses to us in the preceding scripture that the prophet is one of five gifts Jesus gave to the Church for its maturing and equipping. **I submit that this scripture (Eph. 4:11, 12) alone substantiates the need and purpose of the ministry gift of prophet.** As I sketch the N.T. prophet in the next chapter, I trust that it will continue to demonstrate the necessity of this ministry gift.

Please allow me to offer you this one thought. If it were possible to bring the Church to maturity with only three of the five ministry gifts working to their fullest potential and acceptance,(i.e. pastor, evangelist, teacher), we should have already seen the second coming of the Lord Jesus! I am not saying that the prophet's ministry is the best, the biggest, the most needed or the most important. I am saying that Jesus Christ appointed **five** ministry gifts to perfect and equip the Church. Not one, not two, not even three or four! It will take all five to wake, shake and equip the army of the Lord. We are moving forward into a new decade when God's ministry gifts must learn to flow together, work together, minister together and respect one another (Rom. 12:5, 6).

In the past, we have neglected the benefits of "team" attitude and "team" relationship. The vitality of the early church was due to Spirit-filled corporality, not Spirit-filled individualism. The work of the Holy Spirit has never been to produce great individuals, but to produce the great corporate "man" of Ephesians 4. **Therefore, Jesus' gift of prophet to His church is an essential, significant, and indispensable component of God's leadership team.**

Let us continue to the next chapter where I will briefly define the N.T. prophet. In doing so, I pray you will continue to gain insight and understanding as to why God is restoring the ministry gift of prophet back to the Church in its full anointing.

CHAPTER THREE

DEFINING THE N.T. PROPHET

Gift of Prophecy
— Office of a Prophet

Sometimes it is best to define a subject by first portraying some of the things it is not. With this in mind, I have listed three of the most common misinterpretations of what a N.T. prophet is.

First and foremost is the common misconception that anyone who prophesies is a prophet. The ability to prophecy is not limited to the ministry gift of prophet. As we see in I Cor. 12:10, the Holy Spirit gives certain believers the gift of prophesy. We also read in I Cor. 14:31 that "ye may all prophecy one by one". There are times when the spirit of prophecy is so evident in a *Saul* church service that literally all in attendance may prophesy. We see in I Samuel 19 that, even when Saul was pursuing David, the spirit of prophecy came upon him and "he stripped off his clothes also, and prophesied before Samuel in like manner...wherefore they say, Is Saul also among the Prophets? Just because a believer prophesies does not make him a God-called N.T. prophet.

Secondly, one who receives dreams and visions or operates in the word of knowledge is not necessarily a prophet. Again, the Bible clearly states that visions and dreams are not limited to the prophetic call (Acts 2:17) and that the word of knowledge is not limited to the ministry of the prophet (I Cor 12:9).

A third misconception is that only a prophet preaches by divine inspiration (without using notes or outlines). This type of preaching can be "prophetic preaching" (a divine message for a particular people at a particular time) and can be delivered through a pastor, teacher, etc.. But this still does not qualify the minister to be called a Christ-gifted N.T. prophet.

What is a New Testament prophet? **The New Testament prophet is a ministry gift, endowed by God with certain abilities or graces. Each of God's ministry gifts have certain areas of divine grace.** Prophets are receivers of revelation and are essential to the establishing of the Body of Christ through confirmation, correction and direction. We can find N.T. prophets operating in any number of different functions. They can be a senior minister at a local fellowship, an associate minister at a local church, possibly a traveling minister, or even a businessman in the business world. Keep in mind that in the Old Testament, Daniel was an administrator for Nebuchadnezzar, Jeremiah was a statesman, Amos and Moses were shepherds, Ezra was a priest and copyist, etc..

On the next pages are listed some of the attributes or giftings of the New Testament prophet, which allow us to recognize this vital ministry gift:

EXHORTING - By definition, the word exhortation encompasses counsel, guidance, correction and motivation.

Counsel - The prophet helps bring the wisdom of God, through divinely-inspired revelation. As an example, the Apostle Paul charges young Timothy in I Tim. 1:18, "This command I entrust to you, Timothy, my son, in accordance with the prophecies previously made concerning you, that **by them** you might fight the good fight."

Guidance - Through the "rhema" word (a word made alive by the Holy Spirit), the prophet speaks the mind of the Lord. This revelation knowledge can give specific direction to churches, businesses and individual believers. As examples: Moses provided direction for the children of Israel, most likely Silas provided direction for Paul (Acts 16:6), prophets at Antioch gave direction to Paul and Barnabas (Acts 13:2) and Elisha provided direction for Naaman (II King 5:10). Let me also clarify, that when it comes to a "directive" prophetic word to the local church, the ultimate responsibility for discerning and acting upon that word, lies with the eldership. As the God given authority in the church, they also stand accountable before God because they have been entrusted with the RESPONSIBILITY of the vision. With the responsibility, automatically comes the burden and authority to judge the word given.

Correction - Whom God loves, He corrects (Hebrews 12:5-7); and He chooses the ministry of the

23

prophet for this function. God spoke to Ezekiel and said in Ezekiel 3:17, 18:

"Son of man, I have made thee a watchman unto the house of Israel: therefore hear the word at my mouth, and give them warning from me.
When I say unto the wicked, thou shalt surely die; and thou givest him not warning, nor speakest to warn the wicked from his wicked way, to save his life; the same wicked man shall die in his iniquity; but his blood will I require at thine hand."

Motivation - The prophet's ministry "charges" the Church (God's people) to move forward in God's'purposes and plans. Through prophetic proclamation and prophetic preaching, the prophet challenges the Body of Christ to move with God. In the Book of Haggai, we observe the prophet Haggai strategically placed by God to motivate Zerubbabel, the governor, Joshua, the High Priest, and the people to rebuild the house of the Lord. Throughout history, we see that God moves a willing people forward through the words of an anointed prophet. (Example - Prophet Moses was used to motivate the children of Israel from a place of bondage to possessing their Canaan land). Today, God is raising and releasing many "Haggai prophets", who are being used to motivate God's "lively stones" to find their proper place in the Church. (I Peter 2:5)

ESTABLISHING - The prophet's ministry is used to establish the church in different areas:

Bestowing Spiritual Gifts - The Apostle Paul states in Romans 1:11:

> *"For I long to see you, that I may impart unto you some spiritual gift, to the end ye may be established;"*

As a method of impartation, Paul clearly reveals in I Tim. 4:14 that spiritual gifts are bestowed through the prophetic utterance and the laying on of hands. Timothy's life and ministry was better established through the channel of prophetic utterance.

Anointing and Activating - We see many, many examples in the Old Testament where God used the prophet to establish His chosen men in leadership positions. (Samuel anoints King David, Elijah anoints Elisha, Moses anoints Aaron, etc.) In Acts 13, we see certain prophets used by the Lord to anoint and release Paul and Barnabas into their ministry calling. Please remember that this anointing and activating is in compliance with the leading of the Lord, and not left to the discretion of man. (I Tim. 5:22)

Foundation Laying - Together with the apostle, the prophet assists in laying the foundation in the New Testament local church. (Eph. 2:20) More will be said about this in Chapter 4.

This is not an all-inclusive list, but I believe you will begin to sense some of the attributes which will be

25

displayed in the ministry of a New Testament prophet. We must remember that no one is a "prophet" just because they label themselves as such. Jesus Christ is the one who sets in the Church those He calls to function in this ministry gift. Every believer needs to know his/her place of function, but spiritual "titles" are not what we build our ministries on. It is the **anointing** and the **fruit** which justifies one's calling.

CHAPTER FOUR

THE PROPHET'S MINISTRY IN THE N.T. LOCAL CHURCH

It has been said that the local church is the "pivotal ministry", in which God is flowing today. In regards to the local church, one of the greatest areas of deficiency has been in the teaching of the prophet's function within the context of the local church. If indeed the local church is the "hub" in which God is focusing, we must come to an understanding of an integral and important "spoke" in this "divine wheel". The prophet's ministry has an essential role in seeing the N.T. local church come to a place of fulfillment and Godly accomplishment.

In the previous chapter we made mention that one of the divine attributes or giftings of the prophet is that of "foundation laying". In Ephesians 2:20, the Apostle Paul states:

"and are built upon the foundation of the apostles and prophets, Jesus Christ being the chief corner stone. In whom all the building fitly framed together groweth unto an holy temple in the Lord."

We see as a biblical principle that many times the prophet and the apostle operated together as a "team ministry" to bring a solid foundation to the Church. In I Cor. 3: 9-11. Paul again states:

"For we are laborers together with God; ye are God's husbandry, ye are God's building. According to the grace of God which is given unto me, as a wise master builder, I have laid the foundation, and another buildeth thereupon. But let every man take heed how he buildeth thereupon."

We see in Paul's allegory a tremendous truth with regards to the foundational ministry of the prophet. In the original Greek language, the word **master builder** is derived from the Greek word **architekton**, which is composed of two words; **archos**, meaning "chief", and **tekton**, meaning "carpenter". Today this word is transliterated into the English language as the word, **architect**, which means - one who produces the blueprint and oversees the initial construction of a building.

Paul, through the inspiration of the Holy Spirit, gives us an excellent insight into one of the main functions of the N.T. prophet in the local church - that of a "master builder". Holding the thought that we are "God's building", and that the local church is an expression of His building, let us go on to see how the prophet "helps to lay the foundation" in the N.T. local church.

To better understand some of the benefits of the prophet's ministry, whether an individual prophet or a

PLANNER

prophetic presbytery[2] in the local church, I have listed a few "graces" displayed by a true N.T. prophet, who is called to minister to the church. *+ pattern*

#1. HE IS A PROPHETIC PLANNER - In order for any successful building to be built, it must be constructed with the aid of a plan (a blueprint). The prophet's ministry is designed by God to assist the local church by **confirming, adding to, clarifying and laying afresh** God's spiritual "architectural design". The prophet's ministry aids the local leadership by confirming the spiritual plan, and then helps lay out the design for the local church in a prophetic pattern. Another term quite frequently used for this is the "church's vision". One point that must be realized is that every church is not built upon the exact same spiritual pattern. Some churches have an emphasis on the "inner-city", some on the family, some on training leadership and some on teaching, etc.. Many take on the "flavor of the leader", which produces the same "flavor" within the people. This is not necessarily wrong, as God usually does give a man a vision and then places a team around him to see that the vision is fulfilled.

One word of caution needs to said: Many times the prophet will see 10-20 years into the future and the leadership and the people must be patient and wait upon the Lord to see the house built. Just because we can see the blueprint does not mean that the house of

---

[2] See Dr. David Blomgren, Prophetic Gatherings In The Church, p. 67-68

the Lord will be constructed overnight. There must be preparation, gathering of material, training, hard work, much prayer and, most important, solid leadership.

Today's N.T. prophet is a blessing to the local church, because he is God's "seer" for the prophetic plan. In the Old Testament, God used the prophetic office consistently to convey the "plans" for buildings which contained great N.T. spiritual truths. Remember, it was prophet Moses (Deut. 34:10) who received God's blueprint for the Tabernacle of Moses, which portrays the plan of **redemption**. The Lord also used the prophet David by giving him the inspirational plans for the Tabernacle of David, which is now our pattern for N.T. **worship**. David also received the divine plan from God for the Temple of Solomon, which is our N.T. pattern for **worship, government and structure**. Also, a key to King Hezekiah's revival was that the king followed the pattern of worship, as spoken by the prophets David, Gad and Nathan. (II Chron. 29:25)

It is also interesting to note that when the children of Israel built God's habitation according to **His plan**, then His glory was manifested in a mighty way (II Chron. 7:1). The Prophet Haggai spoke in Haggai 2:9 that "the glory of the latter house would be greater than the former". Our generation is on the verge of seeing the literal fulfillment of the ultimate restoration of the temple - the mature Church walking in the fullness of the anointing of Jesus Christ.

Today, like never before, we must desire and seek God's plan for our lives, our families and for our local

EXCAVATOR

churches. God wants to restore to us the fullness of His glory but **we must be functioning according His plans, not our own.** It has been said that it is better to obtain God's plan, which is already blessed rather than make our plan and ask God to bless it.

Through these Old Testament types, we can see that God uses the modern-day prophet as a **"seer-architect"** who can aid the local assembly by revealing any changes or adjustments in their spiritual blueprint.

#2. HE IS A PROPHETIC EXCAVATOR - It is a proven fact that in the construction industry, the higher the building, the deeper the foundation. This principle so aptly applies in the Kingdom of God as Jesus himself said that the greatest amongst us would be the servant of all. To be used mightily by God requires a deep work of the Spirit, whereby God digs the dirt out of our lives and replaces it with a solid foundation of the Word and the fruit of the Spirit. Those who desire to be used by God in a **great ministry** must be available and ready for **great preparation.** Jesus said in Luke 6:48:

> *"he is like a man which built a house, and digged deep and laid the foundation on a rock, and when the flood arose, the stream beat vehemently upon that house, and could not shake it; for it was founded upon a rock."*

No mature ministry will try to build without a proper foundation. Anyone who has ever seen large skyscrapers will readily admit that they are easily visible and grand to behold. Many people desire to have "skyscraper" ministries, but no mature ministry will begin to build without first laying a proper foundation. Consider these important prophetic truths:

1) The taller the building, the more time required for construction.

2) The taller the building, the more susceptible to the "storms of life".

3) Large buildings produce great visibility but they also produce great vulnerability.

4) Taller buildings need greater flexibility to withstand shaking - **flexibility is paramount to stability**.

The prophetic ministry is gifted to look into the Spirit and to help the leadership discern some of the problems in the lives of individual members. Prophets are "spiritual diggers", who love the Church enough to be willing to tell the truth, even when it hurts (Proverbs 27:6).

As an example of prophetic excavating, the prophet helps "dig" through such avenues as prophetic counseling sessions, and/or prophetic presbyteries. During these sessions, the prophet gathers with the local leadership to minister prophetically over the church body. The presbyters will many times sense a weakness in the life of a church member and this weakness will be brought to light, so that it might be dealt with. **The Lord does not reveal our sins to hurt us, embarrass us**

or to harm us. He is a God who loves us enough to chasten us, so that we might be called sons and not bastards (Heb 12:6-8). As God's mouthpiece, the mature prophet will have the wisdom and grace to deliver a word of correction without grossly abusing the children of God.

We would all like to know that our "houses are built upon the rock", but we must realize that **excavation comes before solid foundation**. The N.T. prophet should be a "team member" in the leadership of the house of the Lord, helping to establish the corporate body in a spirit of humility (Proverbs 18:12) and a spirit of responsibility (Mat 25:14-30).

#3. HE IS A PROPHETIC DETECTOR AND INSPECTOR The true prophetic ministry is not motivated by a desire to "look for the sin" in everyone. A true prophet's heart will always be filled with a great desire to see God's people become overcomers. I Peter 2:15 calls the individual members in the Church, "lively stones". Every true shepherd of the Lord desires to see God's people overcome past hurts and failures and to become "lively stones" in the local house of God.

Today we live in a society which is smashing people's lives just as the Babylonians smashed the stone walls around Jerusalem. Many people are attending our churches week after week, yet are not receiving from the Spirit because of past bruises obtained through a crushing experience. Even "Spirit-filled" Christians have been abused to the point that they have a difficult time receiv-

SCARS

33

ing from any leader, regardless of how well he/she can minister.

Let me give you an illustration; **With every "move of God", there are always those who run to the extreme with a truth and who eventually hurt innocent people.** For example, in the "charismatic move", strong, singular rule in the local church became quite prevalent. Around the country, many churches were developed by individuals who assumed leadership positions, but were never called by God and never demonstrated any evidence of accountability. Due to this fact, over the past few years, many churches have dissolved or split because of financial improprieties, heavy-handed rule, sexual misconduct, etc., by the church leadership. The greatest common cause for these situations can almost always be traced back to two main areas of weakness in leadership: - 1) Lack of close relationships and oversight. - 2) Lack of accountability to anyone but themselves. As a result of these "splits" and "ministry failures", many Christians are trying to function in the local church with a wounded spirit. Many pastors around the U.S. are wondering why people come to their churches, but never stay or never get involved. It is because numerous Christians have been "aborted" from the "womb" of a previous ministry experience. Many times they unknowingly do not want to position themselves into another "spiritual womb" for fear that the leadership will "abort the vision" and they will be left to "cruise around" in search for another spiritual house.

I share this illustration with you, as I believe it is a prime example of how the **prophetic detector and inspector**, whether by prophetic presbytery or the individual prophet, can aid the leadership in the local church to bring healing to their members. Today God is raising prophets who can "link-up" with the church leadership to help detect these festering wounds and bring healing. Many times there is a healing balm applied when the prophet speaks a prophetic word over an individual about past hurts. We must remember that the prophet has a Christ-gifted ability to look past the natural and discern the heart of a man.

Before any stone mason uses a stone in building his wall, he carefully looks it over for any defects. He realizes that a crack today could be tomorrow's wall failure. Just as the shepherd in the Old Testament used his shepherd's rod to part the sheep's wool to look for any defects, today the prophet links arms with the shepherd to look into the spirit and detect spiritual defects. Many ministry failures would have been (or can be) prevented through the use of prophetic insight.

Lest someone think I am "prophet pushing", let me say that all of God's ministry gifts can be used to detect hurts and wounds within the sheep, but I believe **God's best is for all five ministry gifts to work together**. No one man or ministry gift knows it all or has it all. Each needs to come to a place of welcoming the strengths of the others. We must comprehend that diversity is God's plan and when it comes to detection and inspection, the

35

PLACER

Lord's prophets have been given a strong measure of His grace.

#4. HE IS A PROPHETIC PLACER - At various times in the local church, the prophetic ministry is utilized to aid the leadership in revealing and confirming the giftings endowed to individual members. The Apostle Peter wrote in his second epistle:

> "*As every man hath received the gift, even so minister the same one to another, as good stewards of the manifold grace of God.*"
>
> II Peter 4:10

God is building His "holy temple" and it is being built with many different kinds of stones, represented by different personalities and different graces.

Again, the Apostle Paul wrote in Ephesians 2:21 that "all the building fitly framed together groweth unto an holy temple in the Lord." Before any "lively stones" (believers) can find their effective place in the local church, they must comprehend the divine enablements with which they have been endowed.

In most congregations, up to 90% of the people have no idea which spiritual gifts (I Cor. 12:1-7) or motivational gifts (Romans 12:6-8) they are to be **stewards** over. One of the greatest challenges to Church leadership in this decade is to help each individual member find their place of function, and then equip them in that area of grace. Unfortunately, in many churches, we have

36

fingers trying to be eyes, elbows trying to function as ankles and toes attempting to be noses. I Cor 12:18 states:

Qualified Instruc order

> *"But now hath God set the members every one of them in the body, as it hath pleased him."*

In order for the army of the Lord to rise up and walk in its inheritance, each individual "soldier for Jesus" must find his/her place of ministry and then not break rank! Paul stated in I Cor. 12 that he did not want the church of Corinth to be ignorant about spiritual gifts. Why did God have Paul write these guidelines? Because God wants each individual member to realize how to recognize, operate and flow in the gifts which He has given to **every** believer.

Proverbs 29:18 also states:

> *"Where there is no vision, the people perish; but he that keepeth the law, happy is he."*

As we look into the Hebrew meanings of a few key words in this passage, we begin to grasp the distinct importance of prophetic insight when "planning and placing" in the local church. The word **vision** is the Hebrew word chazown, which means; a revelation or oracle, and is from the root Hebrew word chazah which means; to mentally perceive, to look, see or **prophecy.** The word **perish** is the Hebrew word para which means; to loosen, make naked or run wild and the word **keepeth**

run wild

Shamar

is the Hebrew word <u>shamar</u> which means; to guard and to take heed. Also, the word **law** is the Hebrew word <u>towrah</u> which means; statute, and whose root word is <u>yara</u> which means; to point out, to aim or to teach. Last, the word **happy** is the Hebrew word 'esher which means; blessed, but it is also from the root word 'ashar which means; <u>to go forward, to prosper, to be level, to be happy.</u>

Combining the Hebrew definitions together, please allow me the liberty of a personal augmented translation of Proverbs 29:18.

> *Where there is not a clear picture or pattern attributed to revelation through a prophetic word, the people of God are <u>loose in their commitment, have no covering, run wild and have no restraint because they are ignorant of their position in ministry and in God's overall plan both personal and corporately;</u> But he that mentally perceives the prophetic plan by; 1) hearing the word of the Lord 2) taking heed to its direction and 3) stands guard to see that it is brought to fruition - blessed and prosperous will he become because he allows the prophetic word to teach him, point him in the right direction and push him forward into God's purpose, plan and position.*

To sum up this scripture, I would say that many Christians never perceive God's purpose, plan and giftings for their lives and due to the lack of revelation, they many times do not find their place of servanthood in the Body of Christ. On the other hand, using the prophetic ministry to gain personal "positional" revelation allows the people of God to be yoked to God's individual purposes. To illustrate this principle, imagine a fast running river during the spring time whose waters are splashing and running wild. Prophetic revelation can act like a dam to restrain the running water and channel it to generate useful power that benefits many people. **Hence, the "restraining yoke" of prophetic revelation is not designed to quench one's call and ministry, but to give it clear direction, application and divine purpose**. We see this demonstrated in Pastor Timothy's life when the prophetic presbytery prophesied and laid hands upon him to give him a clearer definition and understanding of his giftings in I Timothy 4:14.

"Neglect not the gift that is in thee, which was given thee by prophecy, with the laying on of the hands of the presbytery."

The prophetic ministry in the local church helps **reveal** and **confirm** the placement of individual members. Again, this can happen through prophetic presbytery, a prophetic word and/or prophetic counseling. Just as a builder positions a stone to make it fit in the right spot, the prophetic ministry is used by the Lord to properly fit each individual member into his/her proper place of service. **The prophets not only help with the placement of the "lively stones", they also confirm the**

READINESS of the placement. Every "stone" which God uses must be tried to make sure it is ready for placement. It takes time to cultivate tested "lively stones" for even Jesus was prepared 30 years for 3 1/2 years of ministry. God's people must also be properly prepared before the Lord releases them to the fullness of their ministry. Maturity is critical, especially when placing someone in an authoritative position in the house of the Lord. Balance is such an important factor in this realm. We can't expect people to be perfect before they can be utilized, but we also cannot promote believers beyond their level of maturity, lest they be puffed up with pride.

One word of advice: If you are in leadership, do not stifle the people under your care by telling them about serving the Lord without telling them where to get involved. One of the greatest frustrations Christians can face is knowing they have abilities but not an outlet to demonstrate their "graces." We must remember that true Godly fulfillment comes from being a "doer of the word and not a hearer only."

The prophet's ministry can be a valuable asset in the local church to help discern placement and maturity of the individual membership ministries. Working together with the senior elder and the leadership team, the prophet can share valuable insight before any final decision is made with regards to placement or promotion of a church member.

40

CHARGER

#5. HE IS A PROPHETIC CHARGER - As mentioned in Chapter 3, the prophetic ministry is used by God to "charge" the people of God. "Charge" in the New Testament has the idea of a ""military command" (I Tim. 1:18). The prophet's ministry is employed many times by God as a catalyst to motivate the people of God. We see this principle in action during our worship services, when the prophetic word comes forth and the people react with clapping, shouting, dancing and sometimes with reverential awe.

Not only is the prophet's ministry used in the corporate gathering, but it is also utilized in the "leadership gathering". The prophet, through the Word of the Lord, may challenge the leadership to take a daring step of faith. **He is used by God to push the church forward in the Spirit! Without a prophetic spirit, many churches stagnate and eventually dry up spiritually. That is why God usually sends the prophet to "dry places".** *CHANGE*

We must always recognize that God is moving and moving requires CHANGE. Prophetic charging is God's motivator for change, not for **comfort!** The prophetic word has creative abilities, which can change the heart of a people and enable them to step out to do the impossible. Jahaziel's prophecy to King Jehoshaphat and the children of Israel changed their heart from fear to faith. In II Chron. 20:20, Jehoshaphat stood and said:

"Hear me, O Judah, and ye inhabitants of Jerusalem; Believe in the Lord your God, so shall

41

*ye be established; believe his prophets, so shall ye
prosper."*

The children of Israel acted in faith upon their
prophetic "charge" and did not trust in their own
strength to fight the enemy. Because they obeyed their
"prophetic charge" (military command), God utterly
destroyed all the Ammonites and Moabites and blessed
Israel with more spoils than they were able to carry!

One of the greatest aspects of the prophetic ministry
in the end-time-harvest will be that of stirring the hearts
of people to do the impossible. Joel 3:9 states:

*"wake up the mighty men, let all the men draw
near; let them come up;"*

The prophetic ministry in the local church "shakes
and wakes" the people for service through prophetic
preaching and prophetic proclamations. We are the
"Joshua generation", who need to hear the voice of our
Commander and Chief. He is releasing the prophetic
company to the local church in an effort to motivate
God's people forward, as he did with Joshua at the river
Jordan.

In Matthew 10, we note that Jesus prophetically
commanded his 12 disciples to "heal the sick, cleanse
the lepers, raise the dead, cast out devils". They not only
had the power of His name, but they had the authority
of his prophetic command. You can run around every
day with the power of His name, but if you don't have

"prophetic orders", you won't know what to do with the power.

The prophet's ministry blesses the local church by uttering "prophetic charges". These function to restore the zeal, impose a responsibility, activate stewardship and bring the church into a position for attack against the kingdom of darkness. Today, as never before, our churches need the foundational ministry of anointed prophets.

> *"Surely the Lord God will do nothing, but he revealeth his secret unto his servants the prophets."*
> Amos 3:7

IN CONCLUSION: The preceding list is not designed to be all-inclusive, as there are additional facets that prophets can function in with respect to the N.T. local church. I would like to make mention of some practical ways in which church leadership can tap into this prophetic dimension.

First, every church leader should be in faith for the Lord to reveal anyone who is called to this ministry gift function in their church body. One of the key roles of leadership is to recognize the gifts and callings of those placed under their care. If the local church leadership discovers they have a "young budding prophet" under their oversight, they need to see that he/she receives the best possible training from those of a like calling. We have many bible schools whose purpose and focus is to train pastors and teachers, but very few "schools of the prophets". Many "schools of the prophets" are currently in development, and if the leadership is aware of one, they owe it to their young prophet to see that he/she receives proper spiritual training from an older prophet.

Secondly, if the local church is not graced with a prophet within its body, it is recommended that the leadership develop relationship with proven mature prophets. These prophets can be contacted in times of decision and direction for a "witness of the Spirit". Another benefit of strong prophetic relationships is that, quarterly or annually, the prophets can be invited for prophetic presbytery sessions. For an in-depth study on this point, I recommend <u>Prophetic Gatherings in the Church</u> by Dr. David Blomgren.(See recommended reading list.)

Thirdly, those prophets who are in training in the local church should cultivate close, open relationships with the leadership. One of the greatest mistakes of the young prophet is that he/she feels their calling is so "special" that only God Himself can provide input into them. More will be said on this in a later chapter.

Fourthly, leadership need not be threatened by a prophet. Time together - binds together. A close trust relationship needs to be fostered between those of "like spirit" and, if the prophet is not a novice, trustworthy, loyal and faithful, then the leadership should begin to utilize him as the gift he is to their church. Remember, if the Lord purposes to send a prophet to a church, **it will be a reciprocal relationship**. In the multitude of counselors there is safety and the prophetic ministry

44

adds another dimension to the leadership's "sounding board."

In summary, the greatest need we have in the local church today is sound biblical teaching on the prophet's ministry. As with any "restored truth", it takes a certain span of time before leadership and the people accept new revelation. The prophets ministry today is a vital tool in the hands of God to aid the local church in fulfilling its vision.

CHAPTER FIVE

THE TRAINING OF THE MODERN DAY PROPHET

The Lord is calling forth, in this hour, a great company of prophets who will speak even as Joel stated in 2:11 & 16:

"And the Lord shall <u>utter his voice</u> before his <u>army</u>;

"The Lord also shall roar out of Zion, and <u>utter his voice</u> from Jerusalem..."

Those familiar with the armed forces realize that, before troops are sent to battle, they receive rigorous training. Today's "prophetic soldiers" are no different, in that the Lord has a training ground for all His ministry gifts. It is one thing to be called as a prophet, but an entirely different matter to be trained and released to the fullness of that calling. Unfortunately, some Christians think because they have been "drafted", that they are prepared to go to the front lines immediately. Prophets, like pastors, teachers, businessmen, etc., all have a Holy Spirit schooling process to pass through before they progress to separation time (Acts 13:1).

The instant every believer is saved, he/she enters into "basic training" for whatever position in which God has predestined them to serve. Every ministry gift calling (Eph. 4:11) requires in-depth training, because these gifts are an embodiment of our commander-in-chief, Jesus Christ. Even though prophets can operate in divine revelation, or see visions, or prophecy the Word of the Lord, they still need substantial training. We see in I Samuel 19:20 that Samuel started the first "school of the prophets" and was the school's first overseer. Keep in mind that, even though Samuel heard the voice of the Lord at a young age, the Lord kept him in the temple as a servant until he was ready to fully function as a prophet to the nation of Israel.

Salvation in the believer's life produces the seed of the ministry. The call is likened to the birth of the ministry. But before the ministry ever produces fruit, it must progress through the growing phase. The growing phase of one's life is what can be termed, "the training stage".

So, how does God train and equip the N.T. prophet? The type of training a prophet receives is in direct relationship to what type of prophet the Lord is raising. If he/she is a prophet to business, most likely God will expose the prophet to a number of years in the business world. If he/she is a prophet to government, then God will allow the prophet time to develop a knowledge and understanding of governmental matters. If he/she is called to the local church, then the prophet could work as a church administrator, usher, associate pastor, or even as a senior pastor. The mistake made is that people try to fit every ministry gift into concrete categories. God, however, in His omniscience knows how to put the prophet in the right position to see that he/she receives the proper training for the future release.

The Apostle Paul's life is such a clear illustration of proper ministerial training. He knew he was called to the gentiles (Acts 9:15), but a 14-16 year training period in the local church was exhibited before he was ever released to his ministry call (Acts 13). We notice that the Lord provided Paul a broad background in the church before he was sent forth to "apostle" any new works through his missionary journeys. Surely, Paul gained much knowledge and wisdom through his years as a church worker, which he implemented later in the churches he founded. Proper preparation is the greatest key in running the race and obtaining the incorruptible crown (I Cor. 9:24).

Maturity will begin to be evidenced in the life of a prophet when the importance of proper training is realized. Character and courage are attributes that only time and experience can produce. God expects those who speak in His name to not only speak accurately, but to also live a lifestyle consistent with what they speak. II Peter 1: 5 & 7 states:

"And beside this, giving all diligence, add to your faith virtue (moral excellence); and to virtue knowledge; And to knowledge temperance (self control); and to temperance patience; and to patience godliness; and to godliness brotherly kindness; and to brotherly kindness charity."

The above qualities are important in the life of every believer, but take on added meaning for the call of the prophet. At times, a prophet might deliver an accurate word in an area of such as finances, but if the prophet is financially careless, then the Word of the Lord can fall on deaf ears. This principle applies in many areas of the prophet's life, since he/she is God's mouthpiece. It demonstrates the need and demand for every N.T. prophet to live a lifestyle which is blameless.

The prophet's call is demanding in its training. There are inherent obstacles and challenges, which if not responded to correctly, can hinder the development of the prophet. **Time is not a liability, but rather an asset in seeing that prophets are properly trained and equipped to fulfill their call.** All prophet must be willing to submit themselves to the dealings of God, so that **first,** they become men/women noble of character, and **secondly,** that excellence is demonstrated in their ministry. Like Elisha, every prophet should seek to excel in servanthood and in a spirit of true Godly humility. I recommend The Making of a Leader, by Frank Damazio, for an in-depth study on the subject of ministerial training. (See recommended reading list)

50

A great key to understanding God's training process for any prophet is a thorough study of O.T. prophets. I Cor. 10:11, 12 speaks of the Old Testament and gives us a great truth in regards to understanding God's way of training.

> *"Now all of these things happened unto them for ensample; and they are written for our admonition, upon whom the ends of the world are come. Wherefore let him that thinketh he standeth take heed lest he fall."*

As we study the O.T. prophets, we can see that certain experiences were greatly used of God to mold the personality and character of His anointed vessels. Here are a few examples of experiences which brought a demonstration of favorable prophetic development:

Prophet Moses' intercession at the golden calf - demonstration of a willingness to die for God's people.

Prophet Moses at the Red Sea - demonstration of complete trust and obedience to God.

Prophet David dodging Saul's spears - demonstration of loyalty to a higher position, even when being persecuted.

Prophet Elijah confronting the prophets of Baal - demonstration of courage, regardless of the enemies' onslaught.

51

Prophet Elisha's servanthood to Elijah - demonstration of humility and a servant's heart, while in submission to a "father-like" one.

Prophet Samuel's life in Eli's house - demonstration of patience - the ability to wait upon God's timetable before being released as a mature prophet.

Prophet Nathan's relationship to King David - demonstration of a love so great for God, that he was willing to tell the truth to the King.

Prophet Daniel in the lion's den - demonstration of the development of an excellent spirit in Daniel, who didn't defend himself, but allowed God to justify him.

Prophet Jeremiah's ministry to the House of Judah - demonstration of an ability to handle continuous rejection.

As we study the lives of God's prophets, we must realize that God allowed certain experiences to come into their lives, so that the prophet could be developed, and that, hopefully, the prophet would react properly during times of adversity. Many other biblical examples could be given. But I trust you will begin to see that God uses life's experiences as the forge in which He tempers the prophet, so that he might become a vessel of honor. Every prophet must take heed of God's training methods, but also of areas of prophetic vulnerability. Today's "school of the prophets" is not so much a designated place, as it is a divine process. I highly recommend Prophets and Personal Prophecy Volume 1, Prophets and the Prophetic Movement Volume 2, and Prophets, Pitfalls and Principals Volume 3, by Dr. Bill Hamon, for an in-depth study on the subject of prophet training and prophet pitfalls. (See recommended reading list)

> *"When a potential leader harbors leadership ambitions before he is properly prepared, he is courting disastrous failures; adequate preparation coupled with rich experience is the key to successful administration."*[3]

---

[3]Dr. Costa S. Deir, The Potential Leader, pg. 39, 1989, Cityhill Publishing, Columbia, MO.

CHAPTER SIX

UNDERSTANDING PROPHETIC PERSONALITIES

In Chapter 5, it was stated that God raises and trains His prophets in many facets of life. This variety of preparatory background also brings with it a variety of prophetic personalities. If you have seen one prophet, you haven't seen them all. Let us develop this point by contrasting a few O.T. prophets and their ministries.

<u>Moses</u> - Moses' life can be summarized by saying that he was a leader, statesman, historian and legislator. He was a king's son educated in the worldly system of Egypt, yet transformed through a desert experience, and then used in a great deliverance ministry. His personality is marked by one trait which God identifies in Numbers 12:3:

"Now the man Moses was very <u>meek</u>, above all the men which were upon the face of the earth."

<u>Samuel</u> - Samuel was a mighty prophet whose ministry was characterized by a four-fold calling:

1. That of an **intercessor** (I Sam.7: 5-8; 8:6; 12:17,19,23; 15:11)
2. That of a **judge**. (I Sam. 7:15-17)
3. That of a **priest**. (I Sam. 2:35; 7:9)
4. That of a **prophet**. (I Sam. 2:27-35; 3:19- 21; 8:22)

As a prophet, his personality embodied such character traits as courage, discernment and a great heart of compassion for God's people. (I Sam. 7:5)

Nathan - Nathan was a prophet whose ministry was marked by a heart of loyalty. He was a man who loved God enough to bring a convicting word to his own king about his sin with Bathsheba. His personality must have been tempered with great tact, as he still remained one of King David's closest advisers through his entire prophetic career. He was a prophet trained to relate to high governmental figures.

Elijah and Elisha - Even though these prophets worked together as a team, we see a very clear difference in ministry and in personality. Herbert Lockyer writes in All The Men of the Bible:[4]

Elijah was a prophet of the wilderness;
  Elisha was a prince of the court.
Elijah had no settled home;
  Elisha enjoyed the peace of a home.

---

[4]Taken from All the Men of the Bible by Herbert Lockyer. Copyright (C) 1958, 1986, by Zondervan Publishing House. Used by permission.

Elijah was known by his long hair and shaggy mantle;
   Elisha by his staff and bald head.
Elijah was mainly prophetical;
   Elisha's work was mainly miraculous.
Elijah's ministry was one of stern denunciation;
   Elisha's task was that of teaching and winning.
Elijah was a rebuker of kings;
   Elisha was a friend and admirer.
Elijah was a messenger of vengeance;
   Elisha was a messenger of mercy.
Elijah represented exclusiveness;
   Elisha stood for comprehension.
Elijah was fierce, fiery, energetic;
   Elisha was gentle, sympathetic, simple.
Elijah was a solitary figure;
   Elisha was more social.
Elijah had an extraordinary disappearance from earth
   Elisha's death was ordinary.

This is a beautiful contrast of two prophets who ministered to the same people, but who had two different personalities.

Isaiah - His life and ministry portrayed a man who was well-educated and very cultured. He was a poet (Isaiah 1:13; 5:18), a statesman, a reformer and a teacher. Even though he lived during a time of great turmoil, he was an optimist at heart.

Daniel - He was a man born into slavery, yet uncompromising in his actions. He was well-educated as an

57

official of kings and a man gifted by God as an inter-
preter of dreams. He was an administrator and a great
intercessor. He was a man willing to relate to worldly
authority, yet never capitulating to the world's ways.

The list could go on, but hopefully, you begin to
perceive that all prophets are not alike. They do not
wear hairy coats, carry big sticks and wail their prophetic
utterances. God chooses to train and cultivate the
prophet's personality in accordance with the ultimate
call upon the prophet's life. In today's fast-paced, com-
plex society, the Lord is raising prophets for every facet
of life, who are displaying a wide variety of personalities.

CHAPTER SEVEN

REBIRTH OF APOSTOLIC/PROPHETIC TEAMS

In the Church today, there is a rising awareness of the need for greater relationship. Relationship is a vital key to N.T. Christianity and an absolute necessity within the ranks of N.T. leadership. The scripture plainly shows us a great principle for N.T. church government. which we call "team ministry". Team ministry is accomplished when Jesus' ministry gifts work together in harmony and humility, with one mind and purpose, and a dependency upon one another's graces. The key to this model of ministry is **committed covenant relationship**.

One type of biblical team which is being restored to the church is that of the apostle/prophet. We see in Ephesians 2:20, that God set these two ministry gifts into the Body for the purpose of laying foundations. In Acts 13:1-3, we see the Holy Spirit releasing a great apostolic team:

"Now there were in the church that was at Antioch certain prophets and teachers; as Barnabas, and Simeon that was called Niger, and Lucius of

59

> *Cyrene, and Manaen, which had been brought up*
> *with Herod the tetrarch, and <u>Saul.</u>*
> *As they ministered to the Lord, and fasted, the*
> *Holy Ghost said, <u>Separate me Barnabas and Saul</u>*
> *<u>for the work whereunto I have called them.</u>*
> *And when they had fasted and prayed, and laid*
> *their hands on them, they sent them away."*

Apostle Paul and Apostle Barnabas (whose name means "son of prophecy") were released as co-laborers.

Also in Acts 15:22,32 we see the church at Jerusalem sending an apostolic/prophetic team to Antioch to help settle a dispute concerning circumcision.

> *"Then pleased it the apostles and elders, with the*
> *whole church, to <u>send</u> chosen men of their own*
> *company to Antioch with Paul and Barnabus;*
> *namely, Judas surnamed Barsabas, and Silas,*
> *chief men among the brethren.*
> *And Judas and Silas, <u>being prophets</u> also themsel-*
> *ves, <u>exhorted</u> the brethren with many words, and*
> *<u>confirmed</u> them."*

Later in Paul's life, we see him working in close relationship with Prophet Silas:

> *"And Paul chose Silas, and departed, being recom-*
> *mended by the brethren unto the grace of God.*

And he went through Syria and Cilicia, <u>confirming</u> the churches."

Acts 15:40, 41

The word "confirming," in the Greek, is the word "episterizo", which means "to strengthen" or to "support further." This is the heart of the apostolic/prophetic team relationship and ministry. The apostle and prophet work as a balanced fatherly team to help bolster and serve the local church.

In addition to what we have already covered in Chapter 4, the apostle brings to the team an added dimension of **structure and government.** This type of structure doesn't produce a well oiled "machine", but it produces a healthy and vibrant "man" - the body of Christ. Together, the apostle and prophet work as an "apostolic team" to plant, raise and establish local churches and in the midst of these works, they cultivate proper eldership teams (with one senior elder) who are raised to take the oversight of the planted works. Through this establishing process, the apostolic leadership team identifies, acknowledges and trains those "gifts" located within the local church body. This in turn, helps to further develop a multi-faceted ministry in and through the church body. As "spiritual dads", the team helps discern God's blue print for each individual church with the realization that all churches are distinct due to such factors as culture, locality, the needs of the people, etc. Each particular church is constructed ac-

61

cording to prophetic principles but not with the same exact pattern. As the planted work is established and released, the apostolic/prophetic team can aid the "set-in" eldership (Acts 14:23) in matters such as timing, steps to growth, church government, church discipline, doctrinal disputes, confirmation of future leadership and many other fatherly functions.

As a team with God-given spiritual authority, a father's heart, and seasoned maturity, they can help rectify church difficulties, provide restorative counsel, render fatherly covering (not smothering), and if necessary, temporary church leadership. You might say that the apostle/prophet team can fill the role of "trouble shooters" and/or spiritual consultants with a father's heart in the local church. (Acts 15:36) Given the wide range of their spiritual job description, you can see why it takes a number of years of training before the Lord raises and releases a man to be a part of an apostolic/prophetic team.

Being a fatherly team, they impart to the local church a deep sense of family and purpose through a growing demonstration of committed relationship and servanthood. Like Jesus "the Apostle" (Heb 3:1), this divine team should have a transcendent desire to raise up people under their care which will do greater works than them. (John 14:12) **They become God's activators, motivators, and initiators who lay great foundational truths.** Their authority is not based upon titles or a sense of ownership, but through a spirit of brokenness, humility, a father's caring concern and a willingness for family relationship. It has been said that, "Gifted men can build great meetings, but only broken men can build the church."

This dynamic team of men, (their is no minimum of maximum size), not only manifests the gifting to "plant" churches but they have a heart to **release** the people, government, structure, etc., to the eldership team when the Lord says, "Move on." **The willingness to give away that which has been birthed and raised is a great key to apostolic/prophetic fatherhood.** One sign of an apostolic calling is that it usually births more than it can take care of. There are a number of keys in planting a church whose people will have a willingness to liberate the apostlic team when the Lord chooses to move them to new regions. Here are a few:

#1. As the church is planted and established, the apostolic/prophetic team **builds plurality of leadership at the top.** The people are established with an understanding that the church is and will be led by a "team."

#2. As the church grows, more authority and ministry is **released to the people even while the apostolic team is still physically a part of the work.** (As an example, the apostolic team would allow rising pastors, teachers, etc., to minister in the pulpit while the team sits in the congregation and receives.)

#3. The leadership team continues to wean **pastoral responsibilities** to those who are being raised as future elders.

#4. An understanding is imparted to the people through instruction and demonstration that the established work will not forfeit their "fathers" and be abandoned forever. The local church comes to an understanding that they are a part of something bigger than themselves and that their "dads" are moving on to produce more children in the **same apostolic/prophetic family.** Hence, they are not being orphaned but allowed to grow with continued fatherly input.

As you can see, the apostolic/prophetic fatherly team has a call to pioneer, found, cover and put input into the local church. Churches that turn over 80% - 90% of their people every 2 - 3 years without raising, training, and releasing ministries are not building the Church, they are maintaining a platform for the "pastor's" public ministry. Just because a man constructs a successful church does not automatically suggest that he is called as an apostle. Many times, he might only be a strong leader who has gained much wisdom by being a senior pastor. This does not mean that he is called as an apostolic/prophetic team member who can inspire others with a father's heart. Again, ones calling is not built upon personality but on God given anointing and grace. Sometimes we can discount a man's calling and fail to recognize apostolic/prophetic fathers because of the various "mental qualifications" we expect them to meet. (I.E. - Such as expecting all apostles and prophets to be gifted orators. See the Apostle Paul's response to this in I Cor. 2:3-5.)

We, the Body of Christ, will learn more in the coming years about the function and benefits of apostolic/prophetic team ministry. One of our greatest challenges is permitting the Holy Spirit and the Word of God to change our mind-sets in regards to "team ministry" versus the "pastor-staff" mentality. As the decade of the 1990's unfolds, I believe it would benefit every N.T. church to build **close relationship** with a strong, mature apostolic/prophetic covering - **a team with a heart for God's sheep and a spirit of fatherhood to the local church and its leadership.** Truly, our Heavenly Father wants to restore spiritual fathers back to the Church through apostolic/prophetic teams.

> *"Behold, I will send you Elijah the prophet before the coming of the great and dreadful day of the Lord. And he shall turn the heart of the fathers to the children, and the heart of the children to their fathers, lest I come and smite the earth with a curse."*
>
> Malachi 4:5,6

CHAPTER EIGHT

BEING A PROPHETIC PEOPLE

"and in these days came prophets from Jerusalem unto Antioch. And there stood up one of them named Agabus, and signified by the spirit that here should be a great dearth throughout all the world: which came to pass in the days of Claudius Caesar. Then the disciples, every man according to his ability, determined to send relief unto the brethren which dwelt in Judea."

Acts 11:27-29

This scripture characterizes a prophetic people - a people who not only heard the Word of the Lord through Agabus, but a people who acted upon what they heard. We are becoming the generation who truly believe all that God has said in His Word, with the acknowledgement and understanding of the full restoration of the prophet's ministry.

God can and does speak through many channels, such as dreams, visions, a still small voice, peace in one's heart, etc.. But, we are also coming to recognize and respect that the Lord still speaks through the mouths of anointed prophets. A true prophetic people are a people who possess the maturity to discern a word from God and then act upon that word. They are a people who understand God's various methods of communicating His thoughts, and intents and are willing to accept His "prophetic charges".

As the Lord raises, trains and releases His prophets, we must cultivate a prophetic ear to hear what God is saying. There is a great and mighty army being assembled in which every Christian has an important role.

> *"They shall run like mighty men; they shall climb the wall like men of war;and they shall march every one on his ways, and they shall not break their ranks: Neither shall one thrust another; they shall walk everyone in his path."*
>
> Joel 2:7 & 8

> *"Proclaim ye this among the Gentiles,Prepare war, wake up the mighty men, let all the men of war draw near; let them come up:"*
>
> Joel 3:9

In order to be the Joshua generation, we must possess the spirit of Caleb and Joshua. We must be undaunted by past history and know that God is well able to reveal greater truth to us, so that we might become His bride "without spot or wrinkle". The cloud of God is still moving and we must continue to move with it.

Possibly I have challenged your theology or your mind-set in some way. Most likely you are thinking, "But there are dangers to the present rise of the prophetic!" Yes, there are dangers, but moving on with God always demands risk and warfare. To keep us on track, we must make every effort to maintain a balance between moving in the Spirit and the teaching of the Word. If we only rely upon "supernatural revelations", then we become susceptible to the failures of the past. We see these failures aptly demonstrated in the early 1950's when so many of God's servants built their callings on their gifts without the teaching of sound biblical doctrine. As an example, King Asa was given revelation of this weakness in his ministry when Azariah, the son of Obed prophesied:

> *"And he went out to meet Asa, and said unto him, Hear me, Asa, and all Judah and Benjamin; the Lord is with you, while ye be with him; and if ye forsake him, he will forsake you. Now for a long season Israel hath been without the true God, and without a teaching priest, and without the law."*
> II Chronicles 15:2-3

Judah was growing steadily colder in their response to God and the prophetic word conveys to them that they had forsaken the teaching ministry of the law of God. We can minimize "prophetic casualties" while pushing forward into greater truth, if we continue to hold fast to sound doctrine.

We have been called as an army of overcomers and the prophets are coming to help raise, train and release this mighty army. Our generation is being challenged to change. Let us accept this challenge and go on to fulfill God's destiny for our lives.

"...would that all the Lord's people were prophets, and that the Lord would put his spirit upon them!"
                                        Numbers 11:29

RECOMMENDED READING LIST

1. Prophets and Personal Prophecy Volume 1, Prophets and the Prophetic Movement Volume 2, and Prophets, Pitfalls and Principals Volume 3, by Dr. Bill Hamon, 1987, 1990, 1991, (Destiny Image, Shippensburg, PA)

2. Prophetic Gatherings in the Church by Dr. David Blomgren, 1979, (Bible Temple Publications, Portland OR)

3. The Making of a Leader by Frank Damazio, 1980, (Bible Temple Publications, Portland, OR)

4. Team Ministry by Dick Iverson with Ray Grant, 1984, (Bible Temple Publications, Portland, OR)

5. The Eternal Church by Dr. Bill Hamon, 1981, (Christian International, Pt. Washington, FL)

6. Developing the Prophetic Ministry by Frank Damazio, 1983, (Trilogy Productions, Inc., Portland, OR)

7. The Tabernacle of David by Kevin J. Conner, 1976, (Bible Temple Conner Publications, Portland, OR)

8. Present Day Truths by Dick Iverson with Bill Scheidler, 1975, (Bible Temple Publications, Portland, OR)

9. The Prophetic Song by LaMar Boschman, 1986, Revival Press, Bedford, TX)

71

10. The Master Builder by Dick Benjamin, Jim
    Durkin, Dick Iverson, Terry Edwards, 1985,
    (Christian Equippers International Available
    through Bible Temple Publications, Portland, OR)

11. The Elijah Task by John and Paula Sanford, 1977,
    (Logos International, Plainfield NJ)

12. The Second by Kirby Clements, 1988, (Kingdom
    Publishing, Atlanta, GA)

13. Accountable Men by Chuck Clayton, 1992,
    3757 East County Road, 200 South
    Dillsboro, Indiana 47018